CONSTANTINE

Leaders of the Ancient World

CONSTANTINE

Margaux Baum and

Julian Morgan

ROSEN PUBLISHING

New York

Published in 2017 by The Rosen Publishing Group, Inc.
29 East 21st Street, New York, NY 10010

First Edition

Library of Congress Cataloging-in-Publication Data

Names: Baum, Margaux, author. | Morgan, Julian, 1958– author.
Title: Constantine / Margaux Baum and Julian Morgan.
Description: First edition. | New York : The Rosen Publishing Group, Inc., 2017 | Series: Leaders of the ancient world | Includes bibliographical references and index. | Audience: Grades 7–12.
Identifiers: LCCN 2016030406 | ISBN 9781508172529 (library bound)
Subjects: LCSH: Constantine I, Emperor of Rome, –337—Juvenile literature. | Emperors—Rome—Biography—Juvenile literature. | Christian saints—Rome—Biography—Juvenile literature. | Rome—History—Constantine I, the Great, 306–337—Juvenile literature. | Church history—Primitive and early church, ca. 30–600—Juvenile literature.
Classification: LCC DG315 .M67 2017 | DDC 937/.08092 [B] —dc23
LC record available at https://lccn.loc.gov/2016030406

Manufactured in China

CONTENTS

INTRODUCTION

The third century and fourth century CE was a time of change in continental Europe and the lands bordering it. This was especially true for the Roman Empire, which had dominated much of continent and the surrounding Mediterranean Sea for a few centuries. One of the social pillars of early Rome had been its polytheistic religious tradition. Romans' belief in many gods with control and influence over humans and their world is well known to us now. Worship of such pre-Christian deities, and many of the belief systems that came before Judaism and Christianity, are sometimes known as pagan beliefs.

But change had come and was accelerating with a new religion born of the followers of Jesus Christ. Christianity suffered a long, hard road under the Romans, even as it gained more and more believers. Christians were persecuted by Roman citizens and even officially by some of Rome's rulers for much of the early part of the millennium.

But much would change. In 380 CE, the Roman emperor Theodosius I made Christianity the official state church of the empire. By the early Middle Ages, the great majority of Europeans were

This marble portrait head of the Roman emperor Constantine the Great is on display at the Metropolitan Museum of Art in New York City.

Christians. What had brought about this dramatic religious shift for the Romans?

The answer is Constantine I, also known as Constantine the Great. Born around 280 CE in Naissus, Moesia, in what is now Niš, Serbia, he would become emperor of the Roman Empire and would change it forever. Constantine was the first Roman leader who would identify as a Christian. His efforts would pave the way to making Rome a Christian empire and would influence a distinctly Christian culture throughout the Western empire and its Eastern offshoot, the Byzantine Empire.

In the middle of all this, he would also found the city that bore his name for centuries and would become the seat of the Byzantine Empire, Constantinople, now known as Istanbul, Turkey.

Known as a capable military leader, Constantine would first take over as emperor and later united the Eastern and Western factions as one entity. This was at a time that many people, including one recent predecessor, Diocletian, felt that the empire had gotten too large to be effectively ruled by just one person.

Constantine's accomplishments were impressive, even as he was also known for frequent cruelty and brutality. The Roman system of taxation under Constantine, for example, is said to have brought disaster for many Roman subjects, while some tax collection throughout the empire involved torture and other pressures. In general, Constantine's empire had problems with overspending and finances.

But he instituted many important reforms in government throughout the empire and also pushed a program of building construction that greatly changed the face of Rome and many other cities. His efforts at winning converts to Christianity among his subjects, through construction projects and even through bribery and other financial means, among other ways of proselytizing, changed the face of the Roman Empire and paved the way for the Europe of the Middle Ages to come.

CHAPTER 1

THE EARLY LIFE OF CONSTANTINE

In 284 CE, toward the end of the third century, the emperor Diocletian came to power as leader of the Roman Empire. He had thought long and hard about imperial power and had come to the conclusion that Rome had grown too large and too complex for one leader to have sole power over such a large political entity. He believed this was one main reason for the time of chaos called the Crisis of the Third Century, a war-torn period from 235 to 284 CE during which twenty-six people, mostly Roman military leaders, had claimed the title of emperor. An empire that stretched from the British Isles in the northwest to northern Africa and the Middle East needed a division of power, he believed.

Diocletian thought that this vast empire could be best administered by a few selected officials responsible directly to him but having power on an almost equal scale. These new appointees would replace the former provincial governors, whose appointments had left large numbers of men occupying key positions all around the empire. These governors had far-reaching powers but not much supervision from Rome. Diocletian's intent was to secure the empire's long-term stability by reducing their numbers.

POWER SHARING

In 286 CE, a system called the Tetrarchy, in which four people were to be chosen to share power, was created. First, Diocletian appointed his loyal general Maximian to be Caesar. This term, taken from the name of the great Roman dictator Julius Caesar, took on a new context and came to mean assistant emperor. The senior emperor became known as Augustus, taken from the name of the first emperor of Rome. By the end of the year, however, Maximian had been promoted to the level of Augustus, apparently the same rank as the one Diocletian himself held. The difference was that Diocletian would remain Augustus Maximus, or

This is the facade of San Marco Cathedral in Venice, Italy, which depicts the group of four Roman rulers who together made up the tetrarchy that ruled the Roman Empire.

Senior Augustus, holding rank above Maximian and able to bring him to heel if needed.

Responsibilities were shared between the two men. Diocletian retained control over the Eastern empire, making his base in Nicomedia (modern-day Izmit in Turkey). Maximian took responsibility for the Western half of the Roman world, running his operations from Mediolanum, or modern-day Milan in northern Italy.

Diocletian's position was designed to deal with potential trouble from the Persian Empire in the East and from the lands near the Danube River in the north. Maximian looked to protect Rome's flanks against the German tribes east of the Rhine River.

Rome itself was not used as an imperial base of operations, a significant indication that Diocletian saw the city as less important than it had previously been. In effect, he saw the heart of Rome's power as being where the emperors were, rather than as just a city in Italy. The mother city of the empire still had an important role to play as a cultural and national center, but its real importance was diminished by this new, evolving system.

After this first division of power, each

Augustus was given a Caesar who would serve beneath him but have almost equal power as an imperial officer.

In 293 CE, Constantius Chlorus became the Caesar of the West under Maximian, making his base at Augusta Treverorum (modern-day Trier in Germany), whereas Galerius became Diocletian's Caesar in Sirmium, or modern-day Sremska Mitrovica, near the Danube in Serbia. Both men had been promoted to senior posts from relatively humble beginnings. Constantius Chlorus was the son of a goat herder from the Danube lands, and Galerius also came from peasant stock in this region. The Tetrarchy was now complete with a full set of four rulers, as Diocletian had designed it. The Roman world would never be the same.

Diocletian's reorganizations extended to all of the provinces, where the authority of the empire was made secure in stages. He spent much of his time on the Danube frontier suppressing the Sarmatians, as well as visiting Armenia and Syria, where he reviewed the fortifications along the frontier. He dealt with a revolt in Egypt personally and then reorganized how the province was governed. In the meantime, Maximian was carrying out similar work in Gaul (modern France), in northern Europe. It was clear that the system of the Tetrarchy allowed for a swiftly moving imperial presence across the empire. This had very positive effects in terms of maintaining order and discipline. By 298 CE there was a general state of peace throughout the empire, strengthened by a building program around the frontiers and an increase in the size of the army. Diocletian was keen to promote Roman traditions and, in particular, military discipline, which helped create unity.

THE EARLY YEARS

At this time, Flavius Valerius Constantine, or, more simply, Constantine, was a young man growing up in the eastern part of the empire. He had been born in Naissus, which is modern-day Niš in Serbia. The date of his birth is not clearly known and could have been at any point between 272 and 282 CE, though we do know his birthday was on February 27. His father, Constantius Chlorus, the soon-to-be Caesar of the West, was probably not married to his mother, Helena, a barmaid. We have very little certain information about how he was brought up, except for some

This woodcut from 1559 shows Constantius Chlorus, the father of Constantine, wearing a laurel wreath crown, a common symbol awarded to victorious military leaders.

details about how he learned the craft and skills of soldiery in the courts of the emperors Diocletian and Galerius. His origins and childhood were not at all what might be expected of a man who would one day became the emperor of Rome.

After Constantius Chlorus rose to his new position as Caesar of the West, family connections became more important to him. He married Theodora, the daughter of Maximian, in order to secure a connection between himself and his immediate superior. After this, his relationship with Helena was presumably broken off in what was clearly a political rather than a romantic arrangement. Constantius Chlorus urged his son Constantine to marry Fausta, another daughter of Maximian. That move would have made father and son brothers-in-law. Constantine refused, though later he would indeed marry Fausta. Meanwhile, Galerius, the new Caesar of the East, married Diocletian's daughter. While Diocletian did not want the succession to be determined by family ties as it had been in the empire's earlier history, he did very much want to tie together the new "family" of Augusti and Caesars, and alliances through marriage seemed the best way of doing this.

THE RISE OF CONSTANTIUS CHLORUS

Constantius I Chlorus, who would rise to the lofty position of Caesar himself and thereby help raise his son to future greatness, was born in a Roman province called Dardania, on the Balkan peninsula, north of Macedonia. He was the son of a humble family, though there are disputes as to whether he was truly the son of a goat herder or from a more noble background. The latter is believed to be an embellishment that served him better politically as he later rose in the ranks of the Roman military and politics.

As a soldier, Constantius later became part of the Protectores Augusti Nostri ("Protectors of Our Augustus"), an elite guard, and also rose to rank of military tribune. Beyond his strictly military honors, he also became *praeses*, or governer, of the province of Dalmatia, adjacent to Dardania. In 288 CE, during the run-up to the official split of power between leadership of the western and eastern halves of the Roman Empire, Constantius became praetorian prefect under Maximian.

Under his leadership, Constantius spent 287 through 288 in conflict against the Alemanni, a confederation of Germanic tribes who often battled with the Romans along their mutual borders.

However, there were other considerations. What if the Western emperors were to get ideas of their own and take matters into their own hands? Diocletian was wary of this, and as an additional measure of security he arranged that Constantine should be retained in his own court in Nicomedia. He would be a kind of hostage who would secure the loyalty of his father, Constantius Chlorus. So Constantine grew up far away from his parents, close to the center of Diocletian's operations in the East.

In 296 CE, he accompanied the emperor on a military campaign in Egypt before being transferred to the court of Galerius, Diocletian's Caesar. In 297, he again went on a campaign with Galerius, marching eastward against the Persians as far as Ctesiphon, or modern-day Taysafun in Iraq. A great victory was won here, and much land was conquered for the empire.

Constantine was a junior officer in the army and was recognized as a promising young man and a successful military tribune. It was the senior Augustus and his Caesar who taught the young Constantine how to become a fine soldier, which was so important to him later in his life.

The Arch of Galerius, a triumphal arch in Thessaloniki, Greece, was built by the emperor Galerius to celebrate his victory over the Persians, part of which is depicted here.

SHIFTING ALLIANCES

The Tetrarchy of Diocletian continued to rule successfully as long as its leader remained in power. However, it is clear that Diocletian himself held it all together by the force of his personality and because he always retained seniority over his partners. His original design for the system held that power should be awarded to the most deserving candidate and not inherited. Also, every twenty years or so the two Augusti would resign in favor of the Caesars, who would take their place. Diocletian decided that he and his co-Augustus, Maximian, should retire from their posts in 305 in favor of Galerius, the new Augustus of the East, and Constantius Chlorus, the Augustus of the West. Two new Caesars were chosen. Severus was a friend of Galerius, and Maximinus Daia was his nephew. It looked as though Galerius was gaining powerful positions for those who would be loyal to him. Unfortunately for him and for the Tetrarchy, his new regime was destined to come under attack from the outset.

The fact was that two people of undoubted ability had been overlooked in the new power structure. They were Maxentius, son of the now retired Maximian, and Constantine, son of Constantius Chlorus. It is likely that this happened because Galerius's influence with Diocletian was so strong that Diocletian had preferred his candidates to any others. Diocletian had stressed that he did not want power to be inherited, so perhaps it was a deliberate attempt to appear impartial, though that is hard to accept in view of the fact that both new Caesars were so close to Galerius.

It was then that Constantine made a move to separate himself from Galerius. Constantius Chlo-

This painting shows Helena, the consort of Constantius Chlorus, and the mother of Constantine himself, and is a depiction associated with her being raised to sainthood.

rus had repeatedly asked for his son to be sent to assist him in northern Europe, and as he was now about to embark on a trip to Britain to crush a rebellion in the north, he asked Galerius again for his son's release.

His colleague agreed, perhaps reluctantly, and Constantine made a mad dash to escape. It is certain that he felt threatened by the combined forces of Galerius and Severus. His journey up through Europe was undertaken with incredible haste as he made use of staging posts to change his horses.

Constantine began to work with his father in Britain and helped to fight against the Picts, the inhabitants of what is now Scotland. After a successful campaign, they returned to Eboracum, which existed in the same site as modern-day York, where the most northern legionary base of the Roman Empire was established. This was a permanent station where the Roman soldiers kept their camp secure and were protected by the confluence of two rivers.

Constantius Chlorus died here of illness on July 25, 306. This was a turning point for Rome, as the soldiers who had served Constantius Chlorus

The emperor Diocletian is memorialized with this marble portrait head, which was excavated in Izmit, Turkey. Diocletian's reforms changed the empire forever.

for many years now saw their chance to make history. They proclaimed his son emperor, seeing him as an obvious and trustworthy successor to his father. Their illegal claim was backed by Crocus, the king of a German tribe called the Alemanni that was serving with them. The principles of Diocletian's Tetrarchy had now broken down, and the system began to disintegrate.

CHAPTER 2

THE CLIMB TO POWER

The main and most reliable ladder to great power in this era of Rome was to ascend through the ranks of the military and become a general. Whether stationed in or near Rome, in adjoining or far-flung provinces, the soldiers in the imperial armies often felt as much or more loyalty to their commanders as they did to the empire itself. Usually, an appointment to be a general of a large army was highly sought. This gave the generals in question the most power and highest authority. Nearly every contender for the job of emperor had a following, making these men more like self-contained warlords rather than subordinates to the government.

After Constantine's sudden and unexpected promotion, his acceptance by the other emperors could by no means be taken for granted. But his leadership of his father's troops guaranteed that at least his claims would be heard. He wrote to Galerius to explain what had happened in York, and he must have been a little disappointed, though perhaps not surprised, to be told that the senior Augustus could not accept his new status. Instead, Galerius said he would recognize Constantine as Caesar, serving under his own appointee, Severus. This was a good compromise, at least in the short term. Constantine became Caesar and Severus became Augustus, and for a while it seemed that things were working out to everyone's satisfaction.

BREAKDOWN OF THE SYSTEM

But this was an illusion, and the main obstacle to the empire's stability came from Rome itself. In October of 306, Maximian, who had been compelled by Diocletian to retire, stated his open support for his son Maxentius, who rose up and promoted himself as a new emperor in Rome.

Maximian also stated that he was emperor again, and both he and his son claimed the status of an Augustus rather than Caesar. Their support came from the praetorian guards, the protectors and per-

This weathered marble bust, curently on display at an archaeological museum in Milan, Italy, portrays Maximiam, who was co-emperor from 286 to 305.

sonal bodyguards of the emperors. They also had considerable popular support in Rome, where the citizens were increasingly concerned about their declining role in the running of the empire. From the original Tetrarchy, the Roman world had gone to having six emperors, though the authority of two of them was self-assumed. Maximian tried to consolidate the support of the official Caesar, Constantine, by giving his daughter Fausta to him in marriage and by requesting that he should also become an Augustus. However, it was not until almost one year later that Constantine actually used the title. He was treading carefully, carrying out campaigns along the Rhine frontier against the Franks, the Bructeri, and the Alemanni, but otherwise keeping out of the way of the warring factions of his rivals for power.

FURTHER DIVISIONS

By the end of 307, Maximian and Maxentius had quarreled badly with each other. It appears that each had such high ambitions for power that they could not work together as a team. Maximian sought the protection of Constantine, while Maxentius went it alone.

In response, Galerius sent his co-Augustus, Severus, back to Italy to attack Maxentius on his home turf and remove the usurper from power. Galerius was very upset when Maxentius defeated the attacker and Severus was killed. The following year, in 308, Galerius came himself to fight against Maxentius, but he too failed to overcome his enemy in battle. Throughout the wars between Maxentius and the Augusti, Constantine stayed away from the battle zones, preferring perhaps to wait and see who emerged as victor. Maxentius, whose wife was Galerius's daughter, did not pursue his father-inlaw but remained stubbornly in control of Italy.

At the end of 308, Galerius called a conference in Carnuntum, which is modern-day Petronell, Austria, on the Danube River. He invited all the emperors to attend, with the exception of Maxentius, whose authority he refused to recognize. His proposal was to recall Diocletian to power so that order could be restored, but this was not accepted. Then Galerius suggested that Maximian should resign again, which he agreed to do. The new Eastern Augustus should be Licinius, a friend of Maximian who had not held the rank of Caesar. Constantine, who had been promoted by Maximian,

This coin, minted circa the third or fourth century, bears the likeness of Licinius I, who proved to be both a colleague and rival of Constantine.

now reverted to his previous rank of Caesar of the West, with Maximinus Daia as his colleague in the East. One concession was made: they could all call themselves the sons of Augustus (*filii Augusti*). But this was hardly a solution to the problem of who would really rule. So Galerius incurred Constantine's anger, since for the second time he had been demoted.

Yet soon after the Carnuntum summit, both Constantine and Maximinus Daia adopted the title of Augustus. Once again the Tetrarchy fell apart. Maxentius continued to rule Italy with no support from the other tetrarchs.

By the beginning of 310 CE, Maximian rose up again, creating a rebellion among the supporters of Constantine in Arelate, or modern-day Arles in the south of France. He seized control of Massilia, or Marseilles, but was then forced into submission by Constantine, who came rapidly to the scene. Maximian now committed suicide, realizing that his schemes were doomed to failure.

By now Constantine must have regretted very much his earlier support for his father-in-law, Maximian, and he sought from this point on to distance himself from him. He began to claim that the emperor Claudius Gothicus had been one of his ancestors, which was blatantly untrue. Claudius had won a major victory against the Goths in Naissus some forty years earlier in 268, but he was certainly not a relative of Constantine. The victory had been at Constantine's birthplace, however, which seemed an adequate pretext for him to make

Raphael painted *The Battle of the Milvian Bridge*, a portrayal of one of Constantine's famous triumphs. It hangs in the Hall of Constantine at the Vatican Museum in Vatican City, Italy.

the claim.

After his father's death, Maxentius continued to hold Italy and North Africa, aggravating the problems of the other emperors who sought to remove him from power. His popularity in Rome was still high, as he sought to make his mark by embarking on several large-scale building projects, such as the huge basilica in the Forum and a new Circus on the Appian Way, south of the city. Galerius had more or less retired to his base at Serdica (now Sofia in Bulgaria), when a mysterious illness started attacking him, and worms began to consume the inner parts of his body. His previous campaign of persecution against the Christians was abandoned just before his death in 311, when he issued an Edict of Tolerance.

After Galerius died, the remaining emperors again began to forge alliances, well aware that Maxentius's right to power would dominate all other issues of the day. Maximinus Daia agreed to support Maxentius, while Constantine formed an agreement with Licinius that they would work together to oppose Maxentius and remove him from the scene. It was Constantine who had the most reason to want Maxentius removed, as he had been repeatedly duped by his father Maximian.

So Constantine acted. In a series of swift moves, he invaded Italy, leading an estimated ninety thousand foot soldiers and eight thousand cavalry to victory at Turin, where Maxentius's troops had been shut out of the town. After Mediolanum (Milan) surrendered to Constantine, he advanced to Brescia, where he fought again

The death of Maxentius at the Battle of the Milvian Bridge is portrayed here. Constantine's nemesis was beaten and fell into the Tiber River and drowned.

in person at the head of his troops. From there he continued to Verona, where he fought to cross the Adige River in 312.

Maxentius's armies, led until his death at Verona by the general Pompeianus, were no match for the highly trained and experienced men of Constantine. Constantine kept his troops under careful control when they were not fighting. He wanted to appear as a liberator and not a conqueror of Italy, so his army was ordered not to engage in any plunder or looting. The final battle of the campaign was right outside Rome itself, at the Milvian Bridge that spanned the Tiber River to the north of the city.

Despite the fact that Rome was walled and protected, Maxentius led his forces out beyond these defenses to meet Constantine, perhaps because he distrusted the loyalty of the Romans themselves. This proved to be a costly mistake. He was defeated and drowned in the river.

Constantine had arrived at last in Rome, and his victory was absolute. The Senate of Rome voted him Augustus Maximus and master of the West.

CHAPTER 3

STRUGGLE FOR THE EMPIRE

Both Maxentius and Licinius, the other remaining Augustus, had been anti-Christian. Just as Constantine may have himself been a devoted Christian—even for a while before 312 CE—it has even been theorized by historians that his father, Constantius Chlorus, may have been one himself. Scholars of the period have suggested this because Constantius had abstained from full participation in the violent persecution of Christians pushed by Galerius and Diocletian, occurring before the latter abdicated his title in 305.

Diocletian and Galerius had associated themselves with the pagan gods Jupiter and Hercules while trying hard to suppress Christian influence, as this was seen as a threat to the values of Roman religion. We need to bear in mind that the Christian faith held that there was only one god, discounting as false the entire existing framework of the Roman state religion with all its gods. Perhaps the Romans would have accepted Christianity more easily if they had felt that its followers had also accepted them. Nevertheless, Diocletian carried out a program of cruel and vindictive persecution, under which scriptures were burned, churches smashed up, meetings disbanded, and priests arrested.

In the meantime, hostilities were breaking out in the East as Licinius came into conflict with Maximinus Daia. These two Augusti were in conflict over who should control the Eastern empire, and the marriage of Constantine's half sister Constantia to Licinius made Maximinus Daia realize where lay the support of the Western Augustus.

In 313 CE a battle took place in Thrace, in northern Greece, in

This mosaic of Jupiter, part of the larger House of the Planetarium, is located at the remains of Italica, a Roman colony near Seville in western Andalusia, Spain.

which Maximinus Daia was killed by the forces of Licinius. It appeared that the remaining two Augusti could share power and that the Roman world had at last found peace.

This was reinforced in 313 by the Edict of Milan, in which Constantine and Licinius issued a joint statement to the effect that Christians would no longer be persecuted and that their interests would be protected across the Roman Empire. The edict ensured that there would be freedom of religious choice for all peoples and revoked all earlier restrictions on Christianity.

The two Augusti shared the consulship of Rome in 315. But the truce was an illusion, soon to be shattered by Constantine's deep ambition for more power and his burning drive to be the sole emperor of the Roman world.

Constantine considered Licinius to be in opposition to his new Christian regime. Licinius proceeded to have many of his old political or personal enemies removed in a series of killings. He even had the widows of both Diocletian and Galerius executed.

Christians in his territories were discriminated against in favor of pagans, whereas Constantine

This fresco, located at the Oratorio di San Giorgio in Padua, Italy, shows Diocletian conversing with St. George, whom the emperor would persecute and eventually order beheaded.

CONSTANTINE'S VISION

Constantine sought to use Christianity as part of his own personal propaganda campaign. He claimed that he had seen a sign from heaven shortly before the Battle of the Milvian Bridge. There are different versions of the account, but in one version, Constantine claimed to have seen a cross in the sky bearing the words *hoc signo victor eris*, meaning, "by this sign you will be the victor."

From this time, if not before, Constantine was to link his good fortune with his faith and loyalty to the Christian god. The Chi-Rho sign came into use at this time and may have been painted on the shields of Constantine's soldiers. In this sign, the X is actually the Greek letter *Ch*, and the P is the letter for *R*. So the letters combine to say CHR, an acronym for "Christ," and the symbol of the combined letters resembles the image of a man on a cross. This is one of the earliest known Christian symbols.

Constantine was the first Christian emperor of Rome, and he was about to impose his religion on as many of his subjects as he could. He would do this through a combination of pressure and acommodation, but the empire would be forever changed by his initial toleration of, and later enthusiastic adoption of, Christianity.

attempted to promote and integrate both groups when possible. The Christians were a swiftly growing component of society, still perhaps accounting for only 10 percent or so of the people, but clearly favored by the emperor and his policies.

A plot against Constantine emerged when a man named Senecio was accused of conspiracy. He was supposedly involved with Licinius and the half brothers of Constantine, working to remove the Augustus from power, but the details of the case are hard to establish firmly. However, Constantine had just recently promoted Senecio's brother Bassianus to become a new Caesar, and this rebounded badly against the family. Bassianus was killed, as Constantine showed no Christian mercy at all in taking his revenge.

In 316, matters came to a head. Licinius had allowed public demonstrations to take place in his half of the empire against Constantine, and the Bassianus episode had obviously taken its toll. The two men became openly hostile, with battle eventually breaking out again near Sirmium (modern-day Sremska Mitrovica in Serbia). Constantine led an attack by night and, although he was outnumbered by Licinius, his forces prevailed and his enemy fled. In a vain attempt to retain power, Licinius claimed to have deposed Constantine and appointed Gaius Valerius Valens as a new Augustus. Further battles followed in the valley of the Arda River in Thrace. Licinius was defeated again and fled to Byzantium. It was at this point that Constantine and Licinius became reconciled to each other again, with Constantine's position accepted as that of Augustus Maximus. Valens was first deposed and then killed on Licinius's orders. Constantine now had control of the Western empire, including some of Licinius's former territories in Pannonia and Moesia, whereas Licinius held the East.

A SYMBOLIC UNION

This division would hold, but not indefinitely. For the time being it was confirmed by the creation of three new emperors. Crispus, Constantine's eldest son by his first marriage to Minervina, was made Caesar. Constantine II, Constantine's son by his second marriage to Fausta, and Licinius Licinianus, Licinius's son by Constantia, half sister of Constantine, were also made Caesars.

Two of the Caesars were infants, and Crispus himself was only about twelve years old, so it can be

A Roman official reads the Proclamation of the Edict of Milan, issued in 313, which permanently declared that Rome would be tolerant of Christianity within its empire.

guessed that their contributions were not intended to be great at this stage. The symbolic union of the families was what counted. Constantine now pursued further military campaigns against the Franks and the Goths along the Rhine and the Danube frontiers. His reorganization of the Rhine frontier between 317 and 320 kept him away from Roman politics and civil war for some time.

It was some years later, in 323, that Constantine found himself in the Danube area to repel various raids by the Goths, who had been able to cross the river as it froze over in the winter. Their territory of Dacia, lying on the northern side of the Danube, had been brought under Roman rule by the emperor Trajan just after 100 CE. Hadrian had partially surrendered it back to its tribespeople, but it had been a hotbed of activity, and the Goths themselves had been in rebellion for much of this time. Regular raids into Roman lands had been made for the preceding two hundred years or so. These tribes were undoubtedly quite brave and very dangerous, with a fiercely independent nature and a reluctance to submit to Roman rule. But in military organization, tactics, and equipment, they were seldom a match for their opponents.

Constantine's son Crispus, shown here being given control of a naval fleet, achieved great military success at sea and via campaigns on land before falling out of his father's favor.

There were now also problems in the nearby Sarmatian territory, where the king Rausimandus was conquered by Constantine's troops.

Constantine practiced his own particular style of diplomacy in the area. He vigorously opposed the raids but also engaged in a policy of appeasement that allowed many of the tribespeople to enter Roman territory and receive grants of money and land. Constantine's appeasement policy placed a huge burden on the empire, as it was so expensive to implement. In addition, it did not really guarantee the long-term loyalty of those who were brought under Roman rule by this systemized bribery.

THE FINAL CAMPAIGN

While engaged in repelling the barbarian raids, Constantine found himself entering territory in the Eastern empire that had been allocated to Licinius—and doing so at the head of an army. This was sure to arouse the old problems between them. The situation was made more unstable by Licinius's increasing resentment of the Christian influence spread by Constantine, especially where it reached lands under his own control. In 324 the two men came into conflict with each other. This was Constantine's last war against another Roman statesman, and it resulted in a unification of the Roman world once Licinius was defeated at Hadrianopolis, which is modern-day Edirne in western Turkey.

One leading figure in the final campaign against Licinius was Constantine's first son, Crispus. He was now about nineteen years old and had taken command of the fleet, achieving a notable victory at the Hellespont, the narrow channel that connected the Aegean Sea to Byzantium. This is where Licinius had fled after his defeat at Hadrianopolis. Once again, in an act of desperation, he proclaimed that his general Martinian was the second Augustus and that Constantine had been deposed. This was more or less exactly what he had done eight years earlier, and it was to have similar consequences.

After the Battle of Chrysopolis, near Byzantium, which would later become Constantinople, Licinius was finally defeated. Constantia, who was Constantine's half sister and also Licinius's wife, mediated between the two men. She persuaded Constantine to allow Licinius to remain under house arrest in Thessalonica in northern Greece. However, within a matter of months, both Licinius and Martinian had been murdered on Constantine's orders.

Constantine went further, having the

Erected in 315 CE in the historic center of Rome, the Arch of Constantine still stands today and remains one of the most famous and impressive triumphal arches of antiquity.

ex-Caesar Licinius Licinianus assassinated as well. The boy would have been about eight years old. After these killings there was now only one Augustus in the Roman world, which had been reunited for the first time since Diocletian's power-sharing arrangement first came into being in 296. Constantine had achieved this by repeated successes on the battlefield. Even today, his ability as a military strategist cannot be questioned.

CHAPTER 4

CONSTANTINE REBUILDS

The smoke had cleared in 324 CE with the defeat of Licinius, and Constantine was the last man standing, the sole Augustus. He was now emperor. There was much to do, including trying to reintegrate an empire and political system that had been torn asunder by three decades of struggle. Constantine's main goals at this time were to reunify the Roman Empire and establish order. So many soldiers had been killed, along with others, making this a challenge for the new emperor. Rebellion and counterrebellion had weakened the empire. Rome's neighbor states and peoples on its boundaries were not ignorant of this development. Constantine made it his mission to make sure they could not capitalize on this perceived weakness.

This relief on the Arch of Constantine, called the Hadrian Tondo, shows the emperor Hadrian sacrificing to Apollo and is believed to be from an older, now long-lost monument.

SPREADING THE FAITH

Constantine saw it as his duty to convert his subjects whenever possible, and he did so in many different ways. He knew that many were pagans and that if he moved too harshly or quickly in his imposition of Christianity he would lose their support. So he tried to convert them by making the new religion appeal to people in concrete ways. He built hundreds of new churches throughout the empire, and when he came in conflict with barbarians such as the Sarmatians, he offered them money to accept Christianity and Roman rule.

Conversion also included admission into his armies, which were increasingly filled with Germanic tribes. Despite this, the Danube area in particular continued to cause trouble, as the Goths and other tribes there could not be integrated peacefully and reliably into the Roman Empire. In fact, Constantine's appeal to the barbarians may have been counterproductive, as it cost so much gold to implement and also lost the emperor some of the goodwill of his existing subjects, who had to pay for it.

Constantine built a new bridge across the river at Oescus in 328 to improve access to the territories. He also sent Constantine II to campaign in the area in 332. In 334 Constantine came again in person and claimed further victories against the Sarmatians, assuming the title Dacicus Maximus, which had been what Trajan had called himself some two hundred years earlier. Constantine's achievements had nowhere near the same significance as Trajan's, however, and nowhere near the same financial advantage for the empire.

Ironically, Constantine proceeded to dismantle the successful imperial system of Augustus and abandon it entirely in his own attempt to create something permanent. He did this first and foremost by using his religion, Christianity, as a weapon.

Christianity meant something very different to Constantine than it means to Christian worshippers today. Jesus Christ was not the focus of his faith, and he probably spent only small amounts of time reading the gospels. We have seen how Constantine felt that his victory over Maxentius at the Milvian Bridge in 312 was the consequence of his Christian faith. Constantine saw his god as a provider of victory and success and not as a god who understood mercy or suffering.

In spite of this, the famous Arch of Constantine in Rome, erected in 312, depicts the pagan god Apollo assisting Constantine in his quest. Constantine

A finely crafted and detailed statue, *Mithras Killing Bull* is on dispaly at the Vatican Museum in Vatican City, Rome. Mithras held a special significance for Constantine.

claimed to have seen a vision of Apollo in his early career. Apollo was associated with the sun in pagan religion. The arch also depicts various symbols of victory. The winged figures later gave rise to depictions of angels. The arch refers to a divine spirit that supposedly guided Constantine, though it is not clear on the inscription whether this is meant to be an exclusively Christian spirit. Constantine had also worshipped the god Mithras, and Sol, the god of the sun. Constantine insisted that Sunday be a day of rest, and the god Sol was very much in his thoughts. At the time, Christ's birthday began to be celebrated on December 25, which was also the birthday of the god Mithras. Constantine saw no inconsistency in this and worshipped the Christian god along with Sol, Mithras, and Apollo. In his conception, the Christian god could be cruel as well as kind. Most important of all, Constantine felt that the Christian god was the only religious symbol that offered a chance of true unity for the new Roman order he wished to establish.

MORAL UPRIGHTNESS

One of the demands that Christianity made upon its followers that Constantine took most seriously was its demand for moral uprightness. In 326 Constantine ordered the arrest and killing of his eldest son, Crispus, in Pola (modern-day Croatia) and then had his own wife, Fausta, strangled in the steam bath at Augusta Treverorum (modern-day Trier in Germany). Shortly afterward he enacted legislation against adultery, which may give us a clue as to why both were killed. Perhaps they had been having an affair, though it has also been thought that Constantine was excessively jealous of Crispus's success. Perhaps suggestions were being made that Constantine had reached his twentieth year of power, the time when under Diocletian's

Constantine called the First Council of Nicaea, a gathering of Christian bishops that decided important theological issues, in 325 CE.

rules he might think of retiring. Perhaps Crispus was even thinking of making a bid for power.

The reason for the murders is unclear, and Constantine often expressed regret for them in later life. What is obvious is that his own authority over others was absolute at this time, and as sole emperor he could do whatever he liked. This may have had a corrupting effect on his personality. He was the man who had forced his father-in-law Maximian to commit suicide in Marseilles in 310 and had had his brother-in-law Licinius killed in early 325. His list of crimes was considerable by now, as he often resorted to murder to solve his problems.

Under the new order of Constantine, his court gradually became more eastern in style, as he encouraged others to bow to him and recognize him as the all-powerful ruler of their destiny. He cultivated an image of luxury and opulence, wearing his hair long and using wigs. He adorned himself with crowns, highcrested helmets, and jewelry. His costumes were elaborate, and he surrounded himself with many courtiers. He was keen to have approval and eager to please, but his jealousy and temper were terrible, making it difficult for him to maintain any real friendships. He thought that he was uniquely chosen

THE DEATH OF SOPATER

Typical of Constantine's arbitrary behavior was his decision in 332 to have the pagan philosopher Sopater killed in Constantinople. Constantine claimed that Sopater's pagan magic had stopped the winds from blowing and prevented grain from being imported to Constantinople. In his zeal, Constantine arranged that when he himself died, he would be buried between monuments to the twelve apostles in the newly built Church of the Holy Apostles at Constantinople, seeing himself as a thirteenth member of this group. Constantine continued to advance the cause of Christianity, despite what we may consider his rather un-Christian behavior.

to see visions and bring Christianity to the world. This produced in him a dangerous conviction that he was always right and that whatever he did would be approved of by his god.

A STABILIZING FORCE

There had been a perception before his time that Christians were disloyal to Rome and that their loyalties to each other and to their god were more important to them than matters of state. Constantine did not see this as a threat but as one of the faith's great strengths. Christian unity and the support network Christians had developed through burial clubs and retirement funds were forces Constantine wished to exploit across the empire. He was keen to achieve stability, and he wanted Roman interests to be promoted by the church and state working together. Rome itself was no longer especially important as the center of the empire, but the church was. Christian priests in all Roman provinces were encouraged by tax incentives, as church lands were given tax-free status. Constantine's promotion of Christianity was possible because of a general apathy toward Christians in many parts of the empire. The persecutions of Christians, such as those that occurred under Diocletian, failed to catch on in the popular imagination, as religious tolerance asserted itself among the pagans. Constantine sent his mother, Helena, to the Holy Land at some point after the murders

of Crispus and Fausta, perhaps to seek forgiveness for his actions. She acted as an imperial emissary and sought to retrace the steps of Christ to identify

The Patriarchal Basilica of Santa Maria Assunta, in Aquileia, Italy, boasts this mosaic of the rooster and the tortoise, an allegorical symbol of light defeating dark.

both where he had walked in life and where he was crucified. She toured the land, collecting various relics that she brought back to Constantine. These included bits of the cross upon which Christ had been crucified and some of the nails that had held him onto the cross. This was the beginning of a grand tradition of religious relic hunting, which was to affect Europe for many years afterward. Many of its great churches and cathedrals accumulated the remains of saints, old bones, and ancient artifacts from the Holy Land, creating a kind of medieval industry in exchanging and displaying holy tokens of the past.

Constantine kept tight control over the church, appointing all his bishops personally and maintaining a close relationship with them. These bishops had responsibilities for running the churches in their so-called dioceses, or areas of local control. Much of their work was financial or administrative, and there were as many as 1,800 bishops across the empire, with large, landed estates under their control. Church land was exempt from taxation, so there were great advantages if a wealthy man could secure promotion to the position of bishop. Constantine referred to himself as the bishop of bishops, though this could well have been a reference to the fact that *episkopos*, the Greek word for "bishop," can also mean "spy." He certainly wanted his bishops and priests to know that he was watching them and was involved in their activities.

SCHISM AND THE CHURCH

This was because there were threats to Christian unity that had disturbed Constantine's composure for some time. The first sign of a breakup within the church had appeared as early as 311, when a group of Christians in North Africa called the Donatists had broken away from the mainstream of the faith. They were named after a bishop of Carthage, and they were hostile to anyone who allowed paganism to enter into Christianity, seeking to protect the purity of the faith after the persecutions of Diocletian and Galerius.

It is hardly surprising that they came into conflict with Constantine himself, as he was much more easygoing and inclined to accept pagan deities along with the Christian god. Constantine confiscated their churches in 316, but in 321 he instructed that they should not be persecuted. When the Donatists seized control of a church in 330 in Cirta (modern-day Algeria), he simply ordered that a new church be built and conflict should be avoided.

In Saint Peter's Basilica in Vatican City, Italy, the front entrance bears this detail of the crucifixion of Saint Peter. Peter's burial site is supposedly directly beneath the church's high altar.

The Donatists' problem was bad enough, but much worse was the problem of Arianism. This Christian faction was named after Arius, a Libyan who became a priest at Alexandria. His belief was that the nature of God the Father was not the same as that of God the Son. He argued that since God had existed before Christ, he must have caused Christ to come into being and that therefore his essence was not the same as his son's. Christ was in effect less divine than his father.

This rather complex argument seems almost irrelevant today, but Arianism was to cause huge problems for Constantine in the adoption of the Christian faith across the Roman Empire.

THE FIRST COUNCIL OF NICAEA

As the argument began to engulf the Christian world, Constantine called the first Council of Nicaea (in present-day Turkey) to debate the issues in 325. He summoned three hundred or so of his bishops to attend. Constantine grew more and more impatient with Arius, and eventually the debate came to hinge around the inclusion of one letter in a Greek word: should Christ and his Father be called *homoiousios*, that is, of similar substance, or *homoousios*, meaning of one substance?

The council produced an agreement, called the Nicaean Creed, that stipulated exactly what the Christian belief should be, and this interpretation is still used in Christian churches today. The term "homoousios" was kept. The council thus rejected Arius and his beliefs. In English, the creed contains the words "God of God, Light of Light, Very God of Very God, begotten not made, of one substance with the Father." Arguments as to the exact nature of the Son and the Father probably did not interest

Constantine very much, but he was desperate to have unity within his church, and this is what he attempted to create in Nicaea. He felt that brotherly affection and mutual support should be possible for all Christians, with or without the ongoing arguments of Arius, who was ejected from the faith. However, Arius still commanded some support, and in 327 he was readmitted to the Second Council of Nicaea. He continued to irritate Constantine until his death in Constantinople in 335.

CONSTANTINE'S BASILICAS

One method by which Constantine promoted the faith was through the building of churches around the empire. His churches were called basilicas, and they were often huge halls with pillars separating the central nave from aisles on either side. At the eastern end there was usually an altar and an apse, a curved niche in the wall. Light streaming through a window in the morning allowed the rising sun to spread its rays on the worshippers.

The city of Rome had a particular significance for Christians, as both Saints Peter and Paul had been killed there. So Constantine saw the opportunity to

The Archbasilica of St. John Lateran in Rome originally belonged to Constantine's second wife, Fausta. It was given to the bishop of Rome, most likely around 313 CE.

build churches on sites where the two saints had been buried. The basilica of San Paolo Fuori le Mura (Saint Paul Outside the Walls) was set up on the site of Saint Paul's tomb on the Via Ostiense, and the Basilica of Saint Peter was created in the Vatican Valley, where the tomb of Saint Peter lay, near the old Circus of Caligula and Nero. This was a difficult site to build on as the land had a considerable slope and the foundation had to be leveled before anything else could be built there. A canopy was erected over the monument of Saint Peter's tomb in the center of the basilica.

In addition, Constantine created the basilicas of Saint Lorenzo, Saint Sebastiano, Saint Marcellino, and Saint Pietro. He also constructed the "mother and head of all churches," the present-day cathedral of Rome, the church of San Giovanni, or Saint John, in Laterano. This building was dedicated in 324 and built on the site of the barracks of Maxentius's soldiers, whom Constantine had overcome in 312. Saint John in Laterano was unlike the other churches as it was built inside the walls of the city.

Constantine generally placed his churches outside the city walls. This was not simply an accident. He knew that many of the inhabitants of Rome, especially the older families and the senators, were still pagan in their beliefs, and he did not wish to annoy them by appropriating land in the city for this purpose.

Constantine continued with other ambitious construction projects in the city, and under his rule, the Arch of Janus, the Basilica of Maxentius, the Basilica of Constantine, and a set of baths were built in Rome. Also, the Circus Maximus was refitted. However, Constantine could not afford to be seen as just a builder of churches. In Augusta Treverorum, modern-day Trier in Germany, a huge hall was built as part of the Aula Palatina, or Royal Palace, which, perhaps ironically, became a Christian church in later times and is now one of the most startling Roman buildings in the world.

He also had a major set of baths built in Trier which can still be visited. Other churches were built across the empire, including Santa Sophia, a cathedral at Trier, the Church of the Holy Apostles at Constantinople, and the Church of the Holy Sepulchre at Jerusalem.

All of the basilicas of Constantine have been rebuilt since their original construction, some of them many times, so it is impossible to know exactly what any of them looked like when they were first built. In particular, Rome's leading architects of the Renaissance and the Baroque periods reworked them so much that they are now unrecognizable from their original plans. However, any visitor to Rome will certainly want to see how Michelangelo, Bernini, and Borromini added their fantastic shapes and forms to Constantine's early Christian churches.

CHAPTER
5

SHAKING THINGS UP

The promotion of Christianity and church construction were only part of Constantine's agenda. He hoped to impose radical reforms that he believed would change Rome's political order and prevent the weakness and instability of not only the recent past, but of the past few centuries. Since the emperor Nero died in 68 CE, there were few times when the path of succession had been clear. The ambition of powerful men had won over far more often than those making a dynastic claim—that is, the son or heir of the last emperor inheriting the title. The problem of generals rising up with loyal legions supporting them had sowed much discontent. This instability had been the reason behind Diocletian's system of the Tetrarchy, which he had hoped would prevent upstart provincial governors and generals from seizing power.

This stone relief from Nuremberg, Germany, shows citizens paying taxes during the Roman era. The reforms in taxation Constantine imposed were both sweeping and controversial.

Constantine was not only keen to support the church. He wanted to reform the whole Roman system into a new political order that would relieve the empire of the problems it had experienced for many years. Since the death of Nero in 68 CE, it had been clear that no succession to power was assured and that emperors could be created as easily as one could find ambitious men. There had been relatively few times when an emperor's son had inherited the position by dynastic claim. A succession of army generals had risen up at the head of their legions to claim power by civil war and bloodshed. There is no doubt that this had weakened Rome considerably over the years, and that this is why Diocletian had introduced the system of the Tetrarchy to reduce the chance of upstart provincial governors seizing power for themselves.

However, Constantine went one step further. He identified as the source of the problem the fact that the provincial governors were also army chiefs with considerable autonomy, and he decided to change the way the empire was governed and policed in order to reduce the chance of rebellion. In the first place, he separated civilian matters from military ones, creating *duces* (dukes) who would command armies and provincial governors who had no military role at all.

This meant that political power was split between two individuals, both of whom depended on the emperor for their direct support in decision making. It meant that regional imperial power became divided so that the empire itself could be strengthened. Such, in any case, was the theory. In fact, it led to a much more complex, time-consuming system of

The South Door of the Hagia Sofia in Istanbul, Turkey—once the seat of the Patriarch of Constantinople—is shown. Constantine is on the right, holding a model of the city.

government, where all major decisions would have to take longer.

Constantine also dismantled the praetorian guard, which had existed to protect the emperor and his interests. The guards had served Maxentius, supporting his struggle for power in 306 CE, and indeed the praetorians had created many of their own emperors from the time of Claudius in 41 CE. Constantine continued to use a body of up to five so-called praetorian prefects but changed their role to a nonmilitary one. Prefects who had once acted as personal bodyguards for emperors now served in a civilian guise working as important administrators across the empire.

GOVERNMENT EXPANSION

Constantine proceeded to create various new posts, developing a civil service that offered many new career opportunities. He had a series of personal *comites*, or counts, who took on a variety of responsibilities. A count of his private purse handled imperial revenues, while a count of religious donations handled church monies. A new master of the offices (*magister officiorum*) controlled the new,

HANDICAPPING THE SENATE

The Senate was the ancient body of government in Rome, and it had existed since the city's earliest history some one thousand years before. Constantine did not want its interference in his new order, but he saw it as a recruiting ground for his growing body of officials and increased the number of senators from around six hundred to two thousand.

This watered down the Senate's authority, while at the same time enabled Constantine to claim credit for enhancing its size. Again, his policy seems to have been that of divide and rule. From the members of the Senate he recruited a committee that could act with his authority, which helped the prefects to administer the provinces. Constantine spent a large amount of his time away from Rome and had no particular feeling of loyalty to the city, since he himself came from Naissus and had been brought up for most of his youth in the Eastern empire.

Under him, the city was in no real sense the political center of the empire, so the downgrading of the Senate was of little real significance. He certainly did not want to spend his time dealing with its disapproval of his policies, his faith, or himself.

major departments and was given responsibility for many of the other counts and dukes beneath him.

Constantine kept a close eye on things, however, and a new body of imperial spies was set up to report directly to him. These agents were deployed all across the empire. The counts were supported directly by Constantine, but his loyalties could shift easily in this new climate of distrust and fear, especially if the agents worked to change it.

In addition to the officers mentioned above, tax collectors became increasingly feared in the empire. As the tax burden was increased on the provinces, those from whom the money was collected would adopt all kinds of methods to avoid paying ruinous sums of money to the treasury. Corruption was inevitable, and it entered every level of Constantine's new order. As so many people tried to avoid paying taxes, restrictions on their personal movement and that of their families were employed to increase the agents' control.

Constantine's policy of restriction meant that family jobs were inherited and movement within the empire was forbidden. So if your father was a pork butcher, you would become a pork butcher, and retired army veterans who had sons were obliged to send them to serve in the same legion. Interference and control from Rome was feared, but the empire was so huge that it was almost impossible to exert the same kind of control across all of its provinces. Much of the Roman world began to suffer from a breakdown of law and order. Constantine did his best to stop the corruption and the spread of fear by saying he would deal personally with any citizen found guilty of misconduct. In so large a territory as the Roman Empire, however, that could never have been possible.

A NEW CENTER OF POWER

A center for the empire's administration was needed, however, and if it was not to be Rome, where should it be? During the Tetrarchy of Diocletian there had been four centers of administration. Maximian operated from Mediolanum (Milan, in northern Italy), Constantius Chlorus from Augusta Treverorum (Trier in Germany), Galerius from Thessalonica (in northern Greece), and Diocletian himself from Nicomedia (Izmit in Turkey). Constantine realized that the Western empire was far more stable than the Eastern empire, and that his attentions should be focused more properly there. He considered his options carefully. He wanted to have a base from where he could quickly reach the lands across the Danube and cope with any insurgency from Persia, where the loyalty of the local inhabitants could never be relied upon and where rebellions had caused so many troubles throughout Rome's history. Serdica (modern Sofia in Bulgaria) seemed an attractive option, as did Nicomedia itself. But Constantine decided to build a new city for himself at the site of his final victory against Licinius. It would be in Byzantium, an ancient Greek city situated on

the channel known as the Bosporus, which connected the Black Sea to the rest of the Roman world. Indeed, today this is the place where East meets

This atlas shows a map of the Roman Empire in the fourth century CE. Through the fifth century, Rome would lose much territory and split into two distinct political entities.

West, where Europe and Asia are joined. It offered a natural harbor and good transport routes by land and sea. The Via Egnatia was a major Roman road running westward across Thrace, northern Greece, and the Adriatic coast, from which Italy was within easy reach. Grain could be imported to Rome both from the Black Sea area and from Egypt, a major supplier of grain to the Romans.

Constantinople, the so-called city of Constantine, was founded in 326 CE. Constantine promoted it as hard as he dared, luring Romans to it with promises of free grain and land. But the established Roman families were reluctant to immigrate to the city as it was very much at the Greek end of the empire. Architects and artists were summoned from every corner of the Roman world. A forum was built, and many new churches and public buildings were erected, though pagan temples were forbidden. Books were imported from Rome and other outposts of the empire as libraries were built, while works of art such as statues were brought in from across the Roman world. Constantine saw Constantinople as a second Rome, though the speed of its growth may have disappointed him. Its population in 337 has been estimated at only around fifty thousand, as opposed to the one million inhabitants of Rome itself. Constantinople had its own Senate of three hundred members, but it did not have all the officials of Rome, such as tribunes of the people or praetors. Constantinople is certainly the most significant of all of Constantine's building projects. It became the center of the Eastern empire and was not conquered until more than one thousand years later, in 1453. Now called Istanbul, it is still an important city and continues to enjoy great importance as a meeting place of cultures.

Constantine paid for his considerable building program of churches and the city of Constantinople by increasing taxation, but also by plundering pagan temples and raiding their treasuries. Gold statues were melted down to make coins as paganism began to feel the squeeze. Pagan sacrifice gradually fell out of favor and pagan worship was banned in Constantinople. Despite this, paganism did not entirely die out, and emperor worship itself continued in some parts of the empire. Non-Christian festivals in Rome continued to be held on a regular basis and may have occupied more than eighty days of the year. We have seen how Constantine gradually supplanted paganism with Christianity and how he realized how important it was to not simply abandon all previous religious practices. The tax advantages of being a Christian must also have helped his cause. Bishops, priests, and church lands enjoyed a tax-free status. However, this policy caused problems since a great number of people were drawn into Christianity for the wrong reasons and revenue was lost as a consequence.

TAXING THE EMPIRE

The main financial problems of Constantine's reign were caused by his own policies. He was exceptionally extravagant in promoting Christianity, in his building program, in maintaining a huge standing army, and in using bribery to award Christian status to conquered barbarians. In the time of Trajan, for example, the revenues of Rome from the conquered lands of the Dacians and Sarmatians brought enormous wealth into the empire, enabling the emperor to build a huge new forum with markets that were to be a wonder of the ancient world. Yet when Constantine did the same thing, campaigning across the Danube to bring the same peoples back under

A small section of the walls of Constantinople (now Istanbul, Turkey) is shown here. The city's famous defenses have largely remained intact since its founding in 330 CE.

Roman control, he not only failed to bring in wealth to Rome, but actually spent huge sums of money in convincing the barbarians to submit. Even more damaging was the set of reforms Constantine conducted within the empire. By creating so many new spies and officials, he was obliged to pay them all and monitor their activities. He also proceeded to divide his armies, creating two types of forces within his sixty-seven legions, which totaled perhaps half a million men. One set of soldiers was allocated to defend the borders, being stationed at the frontier posts of the empire. These soldiers were called *limitanei*, or frontier guards. They were paid less than the second group of soldiers, called *comitatenses*, or escorts. These were positioned some way back from the frontiers, near towns or settlements that they could supposedly protect.

The legions themselves were much smaller than they had been in earlier times. Whereas a legion under Hadrian had around six thousand men, under Constantine this figure dropped in some cases to as low as one thousand. The military reform was expensive and inefficient, since those soldiers who saw more active service on the frontier were actually disadvantaged in comparison to their colleagues, whose lives were much easier. This led to a feeling of unrest on both sides. Yet again, Constantine may have wanted to discourage any threat from the army, but what he achieved was not what he had planned.

The taxation system that had existed before Constantine had been developed by Diocletian and was based on a fixed annual payment determined by the amount of land owned by citizens. Constantine continued to use this system, but he also introduced a poll tax (a tax on each citizen) as well as an extra tax for the wealthy, senatorial class. Penalties for failure to pay were very high, with a fivefold increase of the amount due for late payment and even a death penalty for evasion. Taxes had to be paid in silver or gold, at least for the manufacturing classes and merchants, though they could also be paid in kind—that is, with goods—by some people. All traders had to pay taxes for themselves, their property, and their employees, which led to untold misery.

Taxes were collected every fourth year, when the most brutal methods of collection were used, including torture. Torture was forbidden by Constantine, but it was widespread across the empire, as was the practice of fathers selling children to pay their way out of tax arrears. Constantine also forbade the practice of tax extortion, where the collectors went too far in doing their jobs, becoming criminals themselves, but this too may have achieved only limited success.

Assessments for taxation were in many cases carried out by town councilors called decurions. These men were put in a difficult position, as their judgments often led to the ruin of their townspeople. They were caught between the rich and the poor and were probably detested by both groups. If they were too zealous in collecting taxes, they might incur the wrath of their citizens. If they were too lax in collecting taxes, they feared the anger of the emperor. Their job was also inherited, so fathers passed it on to sons as the generations passed. There could be no escape.

Taxation under Constantine brought disastrous consequences to the economy because so few of the farmers and traders could pay. In some regions of the empire that had been very prosperous until this time, such as Campania in southern Italy, the devastation was unbelievable because so many citizens became dispossessed and bankrupt. This was made worse by the fact that so few of the ordinary people could afford to own gold or silver, in which their taxes had to be paid. Instead, they carried out their day-to-day transactions using bronze coins, which became steadily more worthless and which were not exchangeable for the more valuable coinage. This problem was not new to Constantine's reign, as Diocletian had also tried to legislate against this kind of inflation, creating a new gold standard of sixty gold pieces to the pound weight of gold. Constantine, however, devalued the gold currency again, making the new standard seventy-two pieces to the pound.

Constantine tried to fix exchange rates to avoid profiteering and fluctuations in the value of money, creating an economic regime with the same restrictive practices as his military reforms. His gold coins were used to pay state officials, members of the army, and barbarians, but the ordinary Roman citizens were privileged if they ever saw them, which must have caused more ill feeling. Silver was used for soldiers' pay and for state transactions, as the bronze coins continued to lose their value. There is no doubt that Constantine's monetary policy was extremely damaging for the common man, as more and more worthless coinage entered the marketplace.

CHAPTER 6

THE END OF AN ERA

By 324 CE, when Constantine had finally defeated Licinius, he declared Constantius II Caesar. This was his second son fathered with Fausta. Though he was only about seven years old at the time, he coserved in this role with Crispus and Constantine II. Two years later, as noted, Cripsus died. Constantine the Great's youngest son with Fausta, Constans, was made Caesar himself at age ten in 333.

In 335, Constantine also appointed a fourth Caesar, Delmatius, the son of his half brother. When Constantine died two years after this, power was left to be shared between the four Caesars. Constantine II took the Western empire, with his base at Trier. Constantius II took much of the Eastern empire. Constans took Italy, Pannonia, and North Africa, and Delmatius took much of Thrace and Greece. Each Caesar was allocated a prefect with administrative responsibilities. It seems most peculiar that Constantine should have done this, since he was the man who had done so much to eradicate Diocletian's Tetrarchy and reestablish the authority of a sole emperor. It is one of the oddities of Constantine's reign that on his death the sole emperorship was again abandoned in favor of a power-sharing arrangement. We cannot fully understand his motives for this, though it has been suggested that he had no confidence in any one individual to replace him.

In 334, the province of Armenia was invaded by the Persian ruler Sapor, and this gave Constantine a pretext to wage a new war against Persia. When Constantine died in 337, he was about to start a new campaign of conquest in the East, which may have been partly fuelled by his desire to achieve new Christian victories among the barbarians. Constantine had a passionate belief that his pursuit of conquest was divinely inspired, and he may have found Persia an irresistible target for his good works. But this work was left unfinished.

Shortly before his death, Constantine was baptized in a church near Nicomedia. This represented

CONSTANTINE AND BYZANTIUM

Constantine can be seen in some ways as the last of the Roman emperors, though there were certainly others who succeeded him. However, he was the last to make a major mark on the empire as a whole, and he left a legacy for the entire world by his actions. The separation of the Eastern and Western Roman Empires, and in particular the establishment of Constantinople as a base in the East, incorporated a political and religious reality that continued for more than a thousand years after his death. These events confirm his importance unquestionably and may even earn him another title: the first of the Byzantine emperors.

His adoption and promotion of Christianity across the Roman Empire had implications for world history that cannot be overstated. The impact of Christianity would reach deep into every area of daily life in Europe, from the significance of Sunday as a day of rest to the development of architectural styles, and even the system of monasticism, where monks would live in communities separated from the lives of ordinary people. This in turn led to the development of many places of learning, including universities and schools, as the Catholic Church remained the dominant force in scholarship for more than a thousand years afterward. The organization of the Catholic Church into units such as dioceses run by bishops has lasted right up to modern times. The meetings of the bishops, known as synods, offered a venue for debate and discussion of civil matters, which before this time had been impossible to achieve in a centralized regime such as the Roman Empire.

his final acceptance into the church and was a cleansing experience for him, whereby all his sins would be washed away. It was normal in those days for baptism to be carried out at the end of a person's life rather than at the beginning, as is common now. Constantine had not wanted to be baptized earlier, as he believed that any freshly committed sins would not be wiped out after the ritual. For the ceremony he was naked, and from this time on Constantine wore white clothing and no longer put on his imperial robes. Within a matter of weeks, he died, on May 22, 337 CE. His body was taken to Constantinople and laid out in the Church of the Holy Apostles, as had been his wish.

A CRUEL STREAK

Constantine was capable of extreme cruelty and barbarism, leading him to even kill several of those close to him. Clearly he enjoyed an absolute authority over his subjects and his family, and this often leads individuals to evil actions. He was superstitious and emotional, and his passionate belief in his god may have tipped the balance of his sanity on occasions. On the other hand, Constantine's acceptance of Christianity did not exclude other religious beliefs, which makes it hard for us to understand quite how his mind worked. Indeed, he seems to have retained some ideas about the gods Sol and Mithras in particular that led him to continue associating Christ with the sun and its worship. Perhaps we need to focus on what he was aiming for rather than what he believed in. His goal was to unite the empire, and Christianity was one of his tools.

A MASTER OF PROPAGANDA

Constantine was a manipulator of information and a master of his own propaganda. Today we hear a lot about political spin-doctoring, where politicians control what is said about them and how their policies are portrayed to the general public. This was something Constantine took very seriously indeed, so there is really nothing new about it today. He managed to emphasize the speed of his journey from Galerius's court to meet his father Constantius Chlorus in Britain, the swift vigor of his attacks on Maxentius's army in northern Italy,

The Baptism of Constantine was painted between 1517 and 1524 by assistants of the artist Raphael, commemorating a milestone in Rome's transformation into a Christian polity.

and his right to be sole emperor because of his invented relationship to the former emperor Claudius Gothicus. His representation of Maxentius and Licinius as anti-Christian may be founded in truth, but then again it could be just another aspect of Constantine's propaganda. The Arch of Constantine in Rome, erected to celebrate his success against Maxentius, uses familiar pagan symbols of Roman victory to celebrate his success, though in other ways he had to be careful about claiming too many victories against fellow Romans in civil wars.

Constantine's struggle to reform the Roman Empire and create a new order resulted in excessive taxation, wide-scale corruption, and a huge increase in administrative systems and bureaucracy. While struggling to strengthen Rome's frontiers, his actions may have had the opposite effect, and undoubtedly he was duped by many barbarians, who simply took his money and scoffed at his weakened regime. More than anything else, perhaps we should see Constantine as a man who never really gave up. While not always successful, he always strove to change things for what he thought was a better way.

THE HEIR APPARENT

Constantine II became Augustus Maximus on Constantine's death in 337 CE. He ruled in the Western empire but was killed in battle by his brother, Constans, in 340 in Aquileia, near Venice, after invading northern Italy.

Constans became emperor of Italy, Africa, and Pannonia after his father's death and extended his rule throughout the Western empire. When one of his officers, Magnentius, led a revolt in 350, Constans was killed in Autun, in what is now France.

Constantius II was the second son of Constantine and Fausta and was emperor from 337 to 361 CE.

Constantius II was probably the most capable of Constantine's sons, and he

This bust of a colossal statue of Constantine is from the Basilica of Maxentius and Constantine, located in the Roman Forum in Rome, Italy.

outlived all his brothers. After taking control of his father's funeral, he became Augustus of the East. He waged war against Magnentius in 353 and defeated him at Mursa, present-day Osijek in Croatia. He remained sole emperor until his death in 361.

HOW DO WE KNOW?

Primary sources for Constantine are of two types. The written evidence comes from various authors, both Christian and non-Christian. These sources are often biased and unreliable but include works by the historians Eusebius and Lactantius. Secondly, there is a wealth of archaeological evidence, in particular that to be found in the city of Rome itself, but also in other outposts of the empire, including Constantinople (modern-day Istanbul) and Trier in Germany, where Constantine had his base of operations for some years. Many Christian basilicas date from the period of Constantine but very few preserve much of their original state.

Augustus After Diocletian introduced the Tetrarchy, "Augustus" was used to refer to either one of two senior emperors and referenced the first ruler of the empire, Augustus Caesar.

Augustus Maximus The superior of the two senior emperors (plural, Augusti).

basilica A rectangular building ending with a semicircular projection on one side, used in ancient Rome as a court of justice or a place of public assembly. Early Christian churches copied this style.

Caesar After Diocletian introduced the Tetrarchy, "Caesar" was used to refer to one of the two junior emperors, referring to the famous Roman dicatator.

circus A large arena enclosed by rows of seats on three sides.

consul The title given to a very senior Roman magistrate, a man who had reached the top of the *cursus honorum*; a largely ceremonial post by Constantine's time.

cursus honorum A series of posts that ambitious senators had to hold in order to rise through Rome's political ranks.

military tribune A term given to a variety of different officials in Roman society, simply meaning a magistrate or official.

pagan A worshipper of the old Roman gods; used to distinguish Christian from non-Christian Romans.

praetor The title given to a senior Roman magistrate, a man who had almost reached the top of the *cursus honorum*.

province An area of the Roman Empire ruled by a governor in the name of the central Roman government.

Senate A body of about six hundred senior statesmen whose authority combined with the emperor's and made up the lawmaking body of Rome.

Tetrarchy A system of rule where command was shared by four people (*tetrarchy* means "rule of four"). It was designed by the emperor Diocletian and first came into full effect after 293 CE.

tribune A type of Roman elected official.

FOR MORE INFORMATION

American Classical League
860 NW Washington Boulevard, Suite A
Hamilton, OH 45013
(513) 529-7741
Website: https://www.aclclassics.org
The American Classical League was founded to foster the study of classical languages in the United States and Canada.

The American Institute for Roman Culture
1101 West 34th Street, Suite 730-174
Austin, TX 78705
(512) 772-1844
Website: http://romanculture.org
The American Institute for Roman Culture works to preserve and protect Rome's extraordinary and unique cultural legacy through education, outreach, and action.

Classical Association of New England
Department of Classical Studies
Wellesley College
106 Central Street
Wellesley, MA 02481
Website: http://caneweb.org
The Classical Association of New England is the professional organization for classicists in New England. It promotes the study of the classical world through the association's many activities and resources.

Department of Greek and Roman Studies
University of Victoria
3800 Finnerty Road

Victoria BC V8P 5C2
Canada
http://www.uvic.ca/humanities/greekroman
The University of Victoria's Department of Greek and Roman Studies offers a wide-ranging, multidisciplinary program combining the study of language, literature, history, and archaeology centered on the ancient Mediterranean world.

Society for the Promotion of Roman Studies
Dr. Fiona Haarer
Roman Society
Senate House, Room 252, South Block
Malet Street
London WC1E 7HU
United Kingdom
Website: http://www.romansociety.org
The Roman Society is the leading British organization dedicated to the study of Rome and the Roman Empire, including history, archaeology, literature, and art. It has a broadly based membership, drawn from over forty countries and from all ages and walks of life.

WEBSITES

Because of the changing number of internet links, Rosen Publishing has developed an online list of websites related to the subject of this book. This site is updated regularly. Please use this link to access this list:

http://www.rosenlinks.com/LANW/const

FOR FURTHER READING

Baker, Rosalie F., and Charles F. Baker. *Ancient Romans*. New York, NY: Oxford University Press, 1998.

Bancroft Hunt, Norman. *Living in Ancient Rome* (Living in the Ancient World). New York, NY: Chelsea House, 2008.

Baum, Margaux, and James Thorne. *Julius Caesar* (Leaders of the Ancient World). New York, NY: Rosen Publishing, 2017.

Boardman, J., J. Griffin, and O. Murray. *The Oxford Illustrated History of the Roman World*. New York, NY: Oxford University Press, 1988.

Cohn, Jessica. *The Ancient Romans* (Crafts from the Past). New York, NY: Gareth Stevens, 2012.

Connolly, Peter, and Hazel Dodge. *The Ancient City: Life in Classical Athens & Rome*. New York, NY: Oxford University Press, 1998.

Everitt, Anthony. *Augustus: The Life of Rome's First Emperor*. New York, NY: Random House, 2006.

Goldsworthy, Adrian. *Augustus*. New Haven, CT: Yale University Press, 2015.

Grant, Michael. *The Emperor Constantine*. London, UK: Phoenix, 1998.

Kulikowski, Michael. *The Triumph of Empire: The Roman World from Hadrian to Constantine* (History of the Ancient World). Cambridge, MA: Harvard University Press, 2016.

Manolaraki, Eleni. *A History of Rome*. Hoboken, NJ: Wiley-Blackwell, 2009.

Petren, Birgitta, and Elisabetta Putini. *Why Are You Calling Me a Barbarian?* Los Angeles, CA: Getty Trust Publication, 2000.

Steele, Philip. *The Roman Empire*. New York, NY: Rosen Publishing, 2009.

Stevenson, Tom. *Julius Caesar and the Transformation of the Roman Republic*. New York, NY: Routledge, 2014

Cameron, Averil, and Peter Garnsey. *The Cambridge Ancient History Volume XIII*. Cambridge, UK: Cambridge University Press, 1998.

Claridge, Amanda. *Rome: An Oxford Archaeological Guide to Rome*. New York, NY: Oxford University Press, 1998.

Eusebius. *In Praise of Constantine*. Berkeley, CA: University of California Press, 1976.

Eusebius. *Life of Constantine*. Oxford, UK: Clarendon Press, 1999.

Cook, S A., et al. *The Cambridge Ancient History Volume XII*. Cambridge, UK: Cambridge University Press, 1999.

Ferguson, John. *The Religions of the Roman Empire*. London, UK: Thames and Hudson, 1970.

Gibbon, Edward. *The Decline and Fall of the Roman Empire*. London, UK: Bison Books, 1985.

Grabsky, Phil. *I, Caesar*. London, UK: BBC Books, 1997.

A

C

D

ABOUT THE AUTHORS

Margaux Baum is a writer and editor from Queens, New York.

Julian Morgan earned his B.A. in Greek studies at Bristol University, England, in 1979. He also earned a master's degree in computers and education at King's College, London, in 1990. He is currently head of classics at Derby Grammar School. Julian has a special interest in software design and has published many programs, including ROMANA and Rome the Eternal City, through his business, J-PROGS. He is a member of the American Classical League's Committee on Educational Computer Applications. He is the computing coordinator for the Joint Association of Classical Teaching (JACT) and has a regular column, "Computanda," in its bulletin. He also runs a training business called Medusa, which specializes in helping teachers of classics use information technology in their instruction.

PHOTO CREDITS

Cover, p. 3 Dave Bartruff/Corbis Documentary/Getty Images; cover background, p. 89 Gail Shotlander/Moment/Getty Images; p. 7 Universal Images Group/Getty Images; p. 12 Universal History Archive/Universal Images Group/Getty Images; p.16 Private Collection/The Stapleton Collection/Bridgeman Images; pp. 20–21, 32 De Agostini Picture Library/Getty Images; p. 23 Vatican Museums and Galleries, Vatican City/Bridgeman Images; p. 25 De Agostini Picture Library/M. Seemuller/Bridgeman Images; p. 29 De Agostini Picture Library/A. de Gregorio/ Bridgeman Images; pp. 34–34, 68–69 Godong/robertharding/Getty Images; pp. 36–37 Private Collection/© Look and Learn/Bridgeman Images; pp. 40–41 Photo © Hilary Morgan/ Bridgeman Images; pp. 43, 98–99 Heritage Images/Hulton Fine Art Collection/Getty Images; p. 47 Private Collection/Bridgeman Images; p. 49 Art Gallery of New South Wales, Sydney, Australia/Gift of James Fairfax 1993/ Bridgeman Images; pp. 52–53 DEA/Archivio J. Lange/De Agostini/Getty Images; pp. 55, 76–77 Alinari Archives/Getty Images; pp. 58–59 Laurie Chamberlain/Corbis Documentary/Getty Images; pp. 60–61 © Niday Picture Library/Alamy Stock Photo; pp. 64–65 DEA/A. Dagli Orti/De Agostini/Getty Images; pp. 72–73 Copyright Frank Smout Images/Moment/Getty Images; p. 79 Werner Forman/Universal Images Group/Getty Images; pp. 84–85 Private Collection/Ken Welsh/Bridgeman Images; p. 101 Hulton Archive/ Getty Images; p. 102 Lipnitzki/Roger Viollet/Getty Images; interior pages background images © iStockphoto.com/kikkalek5050 (sky), Triff/Shutterstock.com (map).

Designer: Brian Garvey; Editor: Philip Wolny; Photo Researcher: Philip Wolny